JIMMIE GUTHRIE
(1897 — 1937)

HAWICK'S
RACING LEGEND

This book is dedicated to Jimmie Guthrie's close family - and in particular his late wife Isabel, a remarkable and gracious lady, to his son Jimmie and to his daughter Margaret. Their help and guidance have been greatly appreciated.

This book published in 1997
Reprinted 2005, 2022
by Hawick Archaeological Society

Hawick Archaeological Society
Registered Charity in Scotland. Charity No. SC016405

ISBN 978-0-9956360-3-3

Produced for Hawick Archaeological Society
by Core 3 Partners Ltd., Buccleuch Mills,
Carnarvon Street, Hawick.

FOREWORD

This book, published by Hawick Archaeological Society, gives an insight into the life of Jimmie Guthrie, a Scottish sporting icon whose life was so tragically cut short.

It traces his career from an early engineering apprenticeship, through serving as a dispatch rider during WW1, followed by the creation and development of a garage business in Hawick with brother Archie. These beginnings led to a glorious career in professional motorcycle racing.

Joining Hawick Motorcycle Club resulted in minor successes in competitive racing, and to being nominated by the club to race in the Isle of Man TT races of 1923. Three years later he was Scottish Speed Champion. Joining the works Norton team as a professional racer meant being regularly away from home, but brought greater success, the rewards of which were ploughed straight into the garage.

Race events were not only riding and racing. At one European event where the might of the German BMW team was evident, their numerous mechanics, amazed at the success of the Norton team, asked my father and Joe Craig, Norton racing manager: "But where are your mechanics?", to which their reply was: "We are also the mechanics."

Having won numerous TT races and European Grand Prix trophies, he was at the peak of his career in 1937 when, while competing in the German Grand Prix his life ended in a horrendous crash. There is still no conclusive evidence as to its cause.

Both Margaret and I are so proud to know he was so loved and admired by enthusiasts around the world.

Jimmie Guthrie, Jnr.

Jimmie powers the 500 works Norton down Bray Hill to yet another TT win — the 1936 Senior.

CHAPTER ONE
THE EARLY YEARS

Jimmie Guthrie was one of Hawick's most famous sons, and in the mid-1930s he was a household name all over Britain, and a lot of Europe as well. So it is both fitting and commendable that in 1997, 100 years after his birth and 60 years after his death, Hawick Archaeological Society should fund this little book. Local teacher John Rogerson and Gordon Small, a Dundee journalist, are honoured to be entrusted with the pleasant task of researching and writing it.

The Society's generosity is doubly fitting, for Jimmie Guthrie's grandfather, who was an architect in the town, was a past President of the Society. Jimmie himself was born at 5 Rosevale Cottage, Wilton, Hawick on May 23, 1897, the third of four surviving children of Jimmie Guthrie and Grace Donaldson. The others were Peggy, Archie and Henry. We will hear more of Archie.

Jimmie's dad was in business as a plumber and brass-finisher in Tannage Close, and was a keen pioneer cyclist. History records that he was the official bugler to the Teviotdale Cycling Club, and a picture exists showing him cycling in white-bearded old age, with his two terriers in a special basket mounted on the handlebars.

In 1909, however, he bought himself a motor cycle - a German NSU 3½hp, the registration number being KS 42. He also became the 453rd person in Roxburghshire to have driving licence. The bug bit, for two years later, he bought a similar capacity Zenith Gradua, and in 1919 acquired a 3hp Royal Enfield for trade purposes. Mr Guthrie died in 1940.

Meanwhile, Archie had become involved with powered two-wheelers also.

In 1919, he bought a 4hp Triumph, the make which had seen sterling service on the Western Front of the Great War which had just come to an end. In 1922, he changed it for a Spark, a make which went into obscurity like so many more. Archie had contracted polio when he was eleven and this had left him lame. So he never went to war.

But brother Jimmie did. He was serving his apprenticeship as an engineer with Wilson and Glenny in Hawick, and in his spare time was keen on sport, particularly skating and shooting. To get more experience as a marksman, he joined the 1/4 King's Own Scottish Borderers (T.A.). They were mobilised for the Great War in August 1914. Pte James Guthrie, No. 785, put thoughts of his home at 61 High Street behind him, and on his 18th birthday sailed to Egypt, and active service.

They ended up at Gallipoli. Attacking the Turkish lines, the Kosbies were caught between two machine guns. Eighteen of the 20 officers were killed or wounded, and 522 of the 680 men. Jimmie was invalided to Malta, rejoined his unit in Egypt, was wounded in the desert, but was subsequently at the successful storming of Jaffa and Jerusalem.

The regiment was then sent to France, and Jimmie transferred to the RE Signals as a dispatch rider, which is where his wife thinks he really got his love of motorcycles. In all this time, he had never been home, and when he did come - in 1919 - Hawick was a very different place.

THE FIRST WINS

One of the first things he did was to buy an army-surplus motorcycle, and he began to spectate at hill-climbs and other events. He had an accident with a Carr's biscuit traveller's car on Howdenburn, Hawick. The Sheriff admonished him, but said that 15 mph was much too fast on that particular corner. What he would've said about the Isle of Man some years later does not bear thinking about. Jimmie was unhurt in the spill, and throughout a long and distinguished career, he seemed to be able to curl himself up in a ball, and seldom hurt himself badly.

No doubt, while watching at speed events, he began to think he could do better than some of the riders. He and Archie became members of the Hawick Motorcycle Club and and his first recorded success was on an AJS at one of that Club's speed hill climbs, held at Lanton Hill, near Jedburgh in June 1922. He won the 350 Experts Barred, was third in the 600 Experts Barred, third in the Unlimited, and third in the 350 Open.

Next year on the same course it was even better. The famous Jock Porter was there. He built his own New Gerrard bikes in Leith Walk, Edinburgh. He was the man of the moment, rode in the Isle of Man TT between 1922 and 1931, winning the Lightweight race in 1923 and the Ultra Lightweight in 1924, both on his own New Gerrard machines.

In 1923, Jimmie beat Jock's record on Lanton Hill by 2 seconds, which is more than it sounds. Later in the day, he set aside his lightweight AJS in favour of a Norton, and was second in the 500 class, second in the 750 and won the Unlimited. He also beat Jock Porter in the 350 Open. In his quiet and modest way, no doubt Jimmie would think that not a bad day's work.

In May of that year - 1923 - he was first equal in a 100- mile reliability trial run by the Hawick Club who, a month later, helped him with his entry for his first stab at the TT in the Isle of Man. In the mid-1930s he would become invincible there, and it would be nice to record a fairy tale win on his first outing. But it wasn't to be. His Matchless/Blackburne broke down on the second lap. He didn't return to the Island until 1927.

The Hawick Club got some interest on their investment by running a show in the town's King's Theatre, which they billed as the official TT film, "featuring the participation of Mr James Guthrie." All very formal !

SUCCESS ON SANDS

It should be appreciated that there were no hard-surface speed events in Scotland until after the second World War when disused airfields became available. Until then racing was confined to hill climbs, grass tracks and racing on the sand. There were grass tracks and hill climbs at Overhall Farm, south of Hawick, but there were many others too, all over the country. The biggest crowds turned up at the sand meetings. Cornering was done in lurid high speed drifts, and there were spills a-plenty.

Among the venues were Cruden Bay in Aberdeenshire, Powfoot near

Annan, and Leven and St Andrews in Fife - where the Scottish Speed Championships were held. Jimmie's first win on the sand was in 1924, at Saltburn, near Redcar, where he beat the great Jimmie Simpson who was already an established TT rider.

The largest race meeting held in the north of England up to that time was at Chevington Sands, Druridge Bay, Northumberland in June 1926. Around 30,000 people turned up, together with the country's top riders. Hardly surprising, for the "North Mail" had put up a trophy and 50 guineas to go with it. A working man's wage would be about £2 a week at the time. The main race was for bikes up to 1000cc and open to all comers, over 15 laps.

Jimmie G had a field day, winning the money and also the 350 Open. This was particularly sweet, because in doing so, he'd whacked the works New Hudsons ridden by the famous Brooklands tuner, Bert le Vack, and Ted Munday. Jimmie had already asked New Hudson for a bike and had been turned down. The result did not pass the notice of the owner of the business, Mr Price.

A month later, Jimmie won the Scottish Speed Championships at St Andrews sands, and his name was becoming known furth of the Borders. Fastest time of the day at the Hawick Club's speed trials near Denholm followed in August, his terminal speed after 1/4 mile being 85mph.

A newspaper cutting showing Jimmie with the New Hudson which he took to second place in the 1927 Senior TT. Note his goggles at the side of his head!

CHAPTER TWO
THE ISLE OF MAN —
AND OTHER MATTERS

And so to 1927, and the start of a meritorious ten-year unbroken relationship with the Isle of Man TT. Mr Price of New Hudson hadn't forgotten and Jimmie was offered works bikes - prepared by tuner Bert le Vack - for the Island races. Hawick was agog. Since 1921 Jimmie and Archie had been in business in their father's old premises as motor and general engineers. Telegrams were posted in the garage window lap-by-lap as the Senior race progressed. He'd never been out of the first six in practice. The crowds round the window were about past themselves with excitement.

Seven laps went by, then Jimmie's name appeared on the leader board at last. " Road wet, foggy, visibility 50 yards. Footrest slack. Passes two leader board riders. Finishes second to the great Alec Bennett (Norton) winner of two previous TTs." Jimmie's average speed was over 66mph. His greatest pleasure, he said, was in having a fag afterwards. There were wild scenes at the Villa Marina prize-giving and "Hawick, Queen o' a' the Borders" was sung lustily by his many supporters.

In order to appreciate this level of happiness for Jimmie, the nature of the man has to be explained. He was a quiet and retiring chap with a gentle sense of humour, but never used two words when one would suffice. After

one Senior TT victory in the '30s, The Motor Cycle said, "Interviewing Mr Guthrie is like drawing four-inch nails out of a piece of oak." He was always generous, often giving away his prize money at local events. At the very pinnacle of his success with the works Nortons, he always said that he was part of a team, and any praise belonged as much to the mechanics as it did to him.

He had guts, and he could "tiger" in adversity, but above all, he had the natural demeanour of a gentleman. It is significant that in Germany in the mid-1930s when nationalism was rife and you would think they would want their own men to win, Guthrie was king. On the day of his fatal accident in far-off Saxony, in a race which everyone knew he should have won, there was virtual silence as the second-placed German rider took the chequered flag. They all wanted to know what had befallen "Gootrie", as they called him.

In the 1933 Junior TT, he came third, had clouted the bank at Hillberry, bending a footrest, and had come off at Quarter Bridge bending some more bits of the bike and skinning his hand and arm. Interviewed, he said, "I found the flies troublesome."

An admirer who lived in the Borders tells of an early-1930s day when he was out on his motor bike. He came up behind what he took to be an older man on a Norton. He thought he'd show the other chap how it was done.

His first TT win, on the 250 AJS in the 1930 Lightweight.

There was a bit of passing and re-passing. Eventually, the Norton rider motioned him into the side. He opened his Stormguard coat and handed the young blade a visiting card. It said "James Guthrie". Smiling shyly, he nicked in bottom gear and rode smoothly away.

The legend grew. He was reputed to have raced the northbound Pullman express on the Newcastleton to Hawick road which ran alongside the track, but didn't repeat it because of the dangers if others copied him.

Mrs Guthrie recounts how Jimmie

used to get up early on summer mornings and ride fast to Keswick for practice. He'd be home in time to have breakfast and be at work by eight. Others got up early too. Recently, Mrs Guthrie was in Langholm with a friend and they were admiring a parked motor cycle. Two old men came up and did the same. One said, "Ye ken, I used tae get up early i' the mornin' jist tae wave tae Jimmie Guthrie."

Archie must take the credit for some of the tuning, and they would test their labours on the A7 north of Hawick. They had the 350 AJS doing more than 90mph, a phenomenal speed at the time. Some local places were similar to the Island and Teindside Bridge and Ancrum Bridge (now by-passed, but similar to Ballaugh on the Island) were practised at racing speeds.

Sometimes he would fall off at an event, and he almost always knew why. At an Overhall, Hawick, grass-track he dropped it, a fact that was pointed out to him by his workshop foreman Alec Waldie, who was also riding. Jimmie said, "I was *put* off when the frame flexed and the chain came off." By the next race meeting, a rear sub-frame had been fitted to prevent a re-occurence.

But of all the folk stories and legends which grew up around Jimmie Guthrie, the abiding picture is of a quiet, modest, good-living gentleman who, once he got his leg over a racing motor cycle exuded uncanny skill and judgement, daring, and good old-fashioned bravery.

The net result, then, of his 1927 Island effort was second in the Senior TT and a retirement on another New Hudson in the Junior TT. But again that year, he won the Scottish Championships at St Andrews.

In 1927, Nortons had won six of the seven major 500cc road races and were going great guns. Yet in 1928, they won only one - the poorly supported French GP. During the winter, the engines had been redesigned and in the practice for the Junior TT, they couldn't pull the skin off a rice pudding. This was particularly unfortunate for Jimmie who had been invited to join the works team which included the current leaders of form, Irishmen Stanley Woods, Jimmy Shaw and Joe Craig. Guthrie was the best-placed Norton in the Junior, and when he came in to re-fuel, was the centre of attraction. This magnified when both machine and rider caught fire, the latter being pursued round the pits by marshalls brandishing extinguishers.

Not surprisingly, Jimmie was a non-finisher in the Senior and Junior in 1928. But that year, we find him abroad with the works Nortons, taking second place in both the Swiss GP and the four-hour long German GP,

The two Jimmies — Simpson (left) and Guthrie, first and second respectively in the 1935 350 French Grand Prix held at Dieppe. Joe Craig is extreme left.

held at the Nuerburgring. He also contested the Ulster and Belgian GPs, again being let down by the poor Norton reliability.

Despite his frustration, there wasn't much option but to stay put for 1929. And although Nortons were going much better, a practice spill - in which the bike was wrecked against a wall - put Jimmie out of the TT. In fact, he didn't figure much on the scene that year. However, his Island purler was to have an effect which would change his life much for the better. In hitting the wall at Greeba, he'd fractured bones in his spine and spent time in traction in Hawick Cottage Hospital.

It was there that he met a pretty nurse, who was quite a bit younger than himself, and their friendship blossomed into romance. She was Isabella Compton of Annan, and they were married in St Andrews Greenhowe Church, Annan, on Old Year's Day,1930. The bride looked charming in a dress of white georgette and lace, and she carried a bouquet of white chrysanthemums and carnations. The best man was brother Archie.

Perhaps because of his unfortunate experience with Nortons, Jimmie changed mounts for 1930, and it turned out to be a wise move. Nigel Spring was a wealthy marmalade manufacturer in Lincolnshire. He was keen on motorbikes and was Norton's unofficial "man" at Brooklands, where records were broken. He'd also been doing a lot of work with AJS, as a tuner. His rider was Bert Denly and together they'd gone all over Europe with these Ajays, knocking spots off world speed records.

Jimmie threw his lot in with Spring (who sponsored four Velocette works riders in the late '40s, including

Freddie Frith to a World Championship in 1949) to ride not only the AJS 350 and 500 racers, but a brand new design of 250 overhead camshaft bike with a four-speed foot-change gearbox. Only one, perhaps two, were ever made, and only in 1930. It was a flyer. In recent years the authors heard tell of it alive and well in the Devon area. It was called "Dopey" because of the fuel it burned.

It was quick and reliable and gave Jimmie his first TT victory - the 1930 Lightweight, at the record average speed of 64.71mph. All round the course came reports of his skill. Tigerish but safe, they said. Unflurried and flat on the tank throughout. But a sharp-eyed observer also noticed the earth jammed into the engine where he'd clouted a bank.

He only did one lap in the Senior before retiring with engine trouble. And in the Junior, he came up from 6th place to 2nd by lap 5 before the engine expired at Crosby. As The Motor Cycle said: "the dashing plucky Guthrie." Later, he also won the 350 German GP, sweetly beating Jimmie Simpson who crashed the works Norton in the heat of battle while lying second.

In 1930 he also rode in the Dutch TT, but retired with engine trouble. Back again at the auld grey toon of St Andrews in July, he and the 350 AJS took the Lightweight Scottish Speed title and second place in the Heavyweight. This event was of national significance, at one time meriting live radio commentary by ex Rudge racer and the then Motor Cycling's editor, Graham Walker. It's said that after his 1930 season Jimmie was offered a two-year contract by a top but unidentified German factory - probably DKW or BMW - but elected to stay riding British.

Riding No1, indicating the previous year's winner, Jimmie hurtles the 350 works Norton down Bray Hill, Douglas during his winning Junior TT ride in 1935. This is the classic "down-to-it" Guthrie style. Note the front wheel pawing the air.

CHAPTER THREE
WORKS RIDER FOR NORTON

Joe Craig, the Norton rider who had resigned because of the bikes' ineptitude in 1928, was back with them as race manager and had the machines sorted out. He and Jimmie always had a great rapport, Craig being one of many who brought his personal car to the Hawick garage to be tuned. So Jimmie was back in the Norton race team for 1931 as junior rider to Stanley Woods, Jimmie Simpson and the meteoric Tim Hunt.

So began the seven-year domination of the European circuits by Bracebridge Street bikes. Between 1931 and 1937, Nortons won 78 of the 100 major 350 and 500 races which they entered. Guthrie himself won 26 TT and GP races, all on Nortons.

In 1931 alone, they won nine of the ten European GPs. Between 1931 and 1937, they won seven Junior TTs, with the first three places in '33, '35 and '37. They were 1st 2nd and 3rd in the '31, '32 and '33 Senior TTs. An amazing record, in which Guthrie played a large part.

It also has to be said that once the camshaft Nortons were sorted out, they were extremely strong and reliable. Rudges were fast but fragile, and in continental events they had to be brought back to Coventry between races for fettling, or fresh bikes taken out. Once Nortons crossed the Channel, they were generally there for the season, occasionally had the

cylinder heads removed for a check, which Jimmie and Craig did themselves. The valve springs were removed after each race, rested for a couple of weeks, and put in again. That was about the extent of it.

The German DKW works team, from the world's biggest bike manufacturer could never win against Nortons at the time. Their race chief said: "Tell me, Mr Craig, why is it that I turn up with a travelling workshop complete with lathes and milling machines, 30 mechanics and 20 bikes, and you turn up with three bikes, no mechanics, and your tools in a little case and you always win?"

When the Norton team travelled abroad, it was all done in style. They went First, with the bikes as registered personal luggage in the guard's van. They stayed in the best hotels. Mrs Guthrie tells of great times in Paris and Spain.

Jimmie had a good TT in 1931, his retiral on an OK Supreme in the Lightweight being more than compensated by fine second places in the Junior and Senior races. Interestingly, although he was on a works 500, the bike was entered by his old friend, Nigel Spring. Interviewed after the Junior, he said, "I didn't have time to fall off too much. The weather was so good, it's a pity the bike wouldn't have done 200mph".

Later, he won the 350 Belgian GP at Spa, and in taking second place in that year's Ulster GP, established a new lap record of 82.43mph. He was third in the 500 French GP and won a 500cc race at the Solitude circuit near

Stuttgart. Again, he cleaned up the Medium and Heavyweight Scottish Championships at St Andrews in July.

Many of the bikes used in Border speed events were tuned in the extensive Guthrie workshops, which was a really high-class and well-run establishment. One particularly fast bike belonged to Alec Waldie who was the Guthrie garage's foreman between 1927 and '32. This was an obscure Hawker Blackburne, which had many successes, culminating in Alec winning the 1931 Scottish Hill Climb Championship, held at Carfraemill near Soutra Hill on the A68. Jimmie himself had a Delage car which had been "breathed on" and the firm's fame was such that cars and motor cycles came from far and wide to be given a bit more puff.

Perhaps being an engineer gave Jimmie a feel for machinery. Certainly

Joe Craig is on record as saying that Guthrie's engines stripped with very little wear, he used as high a gear as possible and never abused the motor. He also said that Guthrie had maximum concentration, particularly relating to corners and braking points, where time was to be made.

The Guthrie business premises covered an area of over 1000 square yards from the High Street back to Teviot Road. There were two showrooms, office, garage, stores and machine shop, which Archie was in charge of. Seventeen men were employed, which included seven apprentices.

The cars of the Border gentry were pampered there and the work which came and went through the doors was of the highest quality. During the second war, Guthrie's did high specification optical work for Barr and

Jimmie (third left) with his pals in the 1929 Norton works team —
Alex Bennett, Jimmy Shaw, Stanley Woods and Jimmie Simpson.

Jimmie aboard a spindly-looking works Norton in the 1932 Isle of Man Senior TT. Note the plug spanner in the top of his boot. A common practice at the time, and a leg-breaker in a spill.

Stroud. The garage was a mecca for local motorcyclists and work would go on often until 11pm. Jimmie always had time to chat to anyone who was keen on bikes.

For reasons which are not the concern of those outside the family, Jimmie's side was not included in the running of the business after his death, control being assumed by Archie's side. Eventually it passed out of the family control altogether. Sadly, in 1997, the site is occupied by a Poundstretcher store.

From an early stage, Jimmie realised the importance of physical fitness. The racing bikes of these times had rudimentary springing and the races - particularly the continental ones - were often over cobble stones. The riders took an awful pounding. The bikes bounced a lot, and when they landed they could be pointing anywhere but the racing line. So in addition to having great skill, riders

were required to be physically strong to control the bikes. Particularly Guthrie, whose style was flat-on-the-tank, thus increasing the pounding.

Four times a week in winter, he would go to Charlie Cotter's gym in Edinburgh, sometimes on the train, but often on a bike, for he always had a Norton at home to practice on. He was an artist at ball-punching but his favourite was skipping. He once did 150 knees-up on one breath which was a gym record. It is further recorded that he hated newspaper reporters and would lock himself in the loo until Charlie Cotter had got rid of them! Fags would be cut down to two or three a day during the season.

In the '30s, Nortons had been experimenting with rear springing and Jimmie had "plunger" 350 and 500 models in Hawick for assessment. Alec Waldie remembers training with Jimmie between Hawick and Langholm, when Jimmie's frame broke and the engine hit the road. Plans to use it in the TT were shelved, and Nortons didn't introduce a spring frame on their racers until 1935.

Practising for the 1932 TT, he had an amazing escape on Sulby straight, at over 100 mph. A flock of sheep poured on to the road ahead. With no chance of braking, he ploughed into them, killing one outright. He managed to stay on, and with the bike little damaged, completed the lap. It was of little avail because he came off heavily on the fifth lap of the Junior, badly injuring his right leg. He managed to restart, but the bike was too bent to continue.

Starting in the Senior against medical advice, and with blood already coming through on his bandaged leg, he began to lap as fast as Woods and Simpson. As the race progressed his leg became progressively useless, but in true hero's style battled through to finish second. Scarcely able to stand, he went off to his hotel and with a ghost of a smile said, "I've never finished a TT without being first or second." He had recovered from his injuries by late July in time to retain his Scottish titles at St Andrews sands, both in record time. It seems he never went anywhere without setting up a new record time!

The "Hawick Express" of August 18 1932 records a "special attraction" of a Hawick v Kelso speedway at Overhall, in which he rode for Hawick without much distinction, but it's remarkable that here was one of the world's top GP stars racing in a local field. It is further recorded that one J. Reid of Hawick had a remarkable escape when his engine fell out !

Such was the superiority of the Norton bikes, that the riders took it in turns to win, particularly on the continent. And Germany was in such a bad economic state that their GP was cancelled. The full four-man Norton team went to the Belgian GP at Spa, and Jimmie, riding to team orders, slowed to let Simpson win, he himself taking second. Jimmie then went home to polish the St Andrews silver and put it back in his display cabinet.

The 1932 Ulster was held in September. Jimmie's Junior Norton was slow to fire up, but after a superb ride in which he broke the lap record at 84.25mph, he took the lead, only to crash. Nortons won 11 of the 12 races in the six major classics they contested in 1932.

MAGNIFICENT

The following year, they took the first three places in the Junior and Senior TTs, with Jimmie G fourth in the Senior. They say the winners of the races were chosen in the Norton board room, not only that, the order in which they would win. Stanley Woods, master tactician, subtle manipulator and the No 1 rider would ensure he had the lion's share.

But Guthrie won the 350 Belgian. However, Velocettes now had their 350 model flying and in the Ulster, Jimmie could only manage second. The Motor Cycle said, "Guthrie rode magnificently against hopeless odds, to finish with his hands blistered in a most horrible manner." He was second in the Swedish Junior in which team mate Hunt crashed so heavily that he never raced again, and the Swedish rider involved was killed.

By then it was late in the season, but there was still the Spanish GP. Craig and Jimmie flew directly there from Sweden. A remarkably innovative move when most people had never seen large aircraft, far less flown in one. The circuit was in the town of Castrejana near Madrid and Jimmie won both Junior and Senior races, breaking the Junior lap record seven times and also the 500 record.

All the works riders were in different financial circumstances. Woods was a pure professional and rode for who would give the best deal. In 1935 for instance, while riding for Moto Guzzi, Stanley made £4048 from racing, including £958 for winning the Lightweight TT and £1467 for the Senior. By contrast, riding for the impoverished Velocette factory in 1939, he made £850. Hunt's people were wealthy and he rode for the hell of it. Crasher White who joined the Norton team in 1935 and who died only in 1997, revealed that he could just about double his schoolmaster's

salary of £500 pa. He, like Jimmie, had other means of making a good living, racing was a paying hobby.

In 1934, Woods moved to Husqvarna and Hunt was out. Jimmie G became the number one Norton works rider and it signalled the start of his greatest time in terms of wins. They had lots of road races and road racers in Ireland, as they do to this day, and the year opened with the Leinster 200 miler where Jimmie won the Junior. In winning the North West 200 - again in Ireland - he pushed the 500cc record up to 82.16 mph.

At the TT, Jimmie lost no time in setting out his stall. Of his practice, The Motor Cycle said, "This morning, he gave a display of fireworks that can rarely have been equalled. On Bray Hill he was really frightening.

"How he held the model is a mystery. Altogether, his performance was a staggering one." Needless to say he won the Junior at a record speed of of over 79 mph with a record lap of 80.11. And he led the Senior from start to finish.

The European Championship then was decided on the result of a single race which was at a different venue each year and was part of a normal GP meeting.The title was the equivalent of today's World Championship and there were 350 and 500cc classes.

The 1934 event was at the Dutch TT. With the 500 race in his pocket, Jimmie crashed, breaking his arm. He was lugged away on a wheeled stretcher, towed by a motor bike. He

was fit in time for the Ulster in the autumn, but fell off yet again on the first lap when leading the Senior. He went into a ditch, rebounded into the middle of the road, where his fallen bike fetched off 10 other riders.

A chastened Jimmie was able to walk to the ambulance station. He atoned in Bilbao, where he won both classes of the Spanish GP, opting for a long open pipe for speed out of the corners, rather than the megaphones Nortons had tried during the season.

That September, the Provost and magistrates of Hawick presented him with a silver cigarette case in honour of his achievements. It had the Hawick and Isle of Man crests on the lid.

The way it was. At the end of the Clady straight in the 1930 Ulster GP. Charlie Dodson (Sunbeam) leads Stanley Woods (Norton) and Jimmie Guthrie (AJS).

Selling motorcycles has always been a highly competitive business, and the publicity gained from wins is meat and drink. And what better time to spring a publicity coup than just before the Olympia Show when everyone else's racing bikes are wrapped up for the winter? Joe Craig and Jimmie took a 500 down to the Montlhery speed bowl, just outside Paris, intending to break some world records. With a huge seven gallon tank full of alcohol fuel, they took the 50km and 50 mile records at 113.23 mph and 113.39 mph. This was the first of three annual visits to Montlhery.

DIGNITY

There was complete revamp of the Norton team for 1935. In came John "Crasher" White and the dashing young blond bombshell of a blarneying Irishman, Walter Rusk - later to die as an RAF pilot in the war. Jimmie was the clear team leader. Johnny Duncan of Aberdeen also made the odd appearance but was never really on the pace.

At the North West 200, Jimmie won the 500 and he also won the Junior TT. On the morning of the latter, the announcer read out a telegram from Hitler sending greetings to the Auto Cycle Union, and wishing every success to the German riders. That year's Senior is recorded as a Guthrie defeat, but it was really a win for the tactics of Stanley Woods, who, by then, had moved to Moto Guzzi. When Jimmie came into the pits on the last lap, they told him the race was as good as his. Craig phoned ahead to the Ramsey signalling station to tell Guthrie to slow and ensure a finish.

He crossed the line 26 seconds ahead of Woods who had started later and who had still to stop for fuel. The Guzzi pit readied the cans, but the wily master-tactician went through without stopping, and eventually finished just 3 seconds ahead of Guthrie. Disaster for Guthrie and Nortons, but Jimmie was one of the first to congratulate Stanley.

Motor Cycling said: "A good fellow Guthrie, and a fine sport. A man who can make a habit of winning yet make a graceful gesture when victory is turned into defeat. Good old Jimmie Guthrie. One wants to grasp his hand firmly, perhaps silently, but nonetheless sincerely."

There was some consolation in that Norton won the team prize, and a few days later, Jimmie won the 500 Swiss GP. Having also raced in the 350 event, he had covered 408 racing miles in a single day. Tell that to today's highly paid racers! Six days later, he won the 500 Dutch TT. Then he and Rusk took the train to the German GP at the Sachsenring, near Chemnitz, where he again won the 500 class.

Within a matter of days, the four-man Norton team gathered for the Belgian GP. Team orders were in force and Jimmie won the 500 class with a record lap of over 90 mph. In the Ulster GP, he rode an astonishing race. Team mate Rusk made a good start, but fell. To avoid him, Jimmie threw his bike up the road at high speed ending up in a hedge, and bending the bike severely.

Kicking it straight as best he could, he set off in pursuit of the leaders - Mellors (FN), Woods (Guzzi), and Tyrell Smith (New Imperial). Putting the lap record up to 95.35 mph, he passed the lot to win at an average of 90.98 mph. It was the first time that a classic race had been won at above 90 mph average, and the pace was so hot that the other three retired.

THE IMAGE GALLERY

Humehall Brae, Jimmie Guthrie (Norton),
Archie Guthrie (Triumph).

Jimmie fooling about with his Matchless at T.T. 1923.

*Jock Porter (New Gerrard). Twice winner of the T.T. at Lanton Hill hillclimb,
behind is G.Black (Norton).*

*Jimmie on his Big Port (A.J.S.) which is on display in Hawick Museum.
Probably 1926.*

*Jimmie (A.J.S.). On the inside line at
Newton Sands 1926.*

*Jimmie (A.J.S.). First place with the third place rider in the 350cc Scottish Championships
at St. Andrews 1926.*

Jimmie 1927. Senior T.T. second place.
(New Hudson).

New Hudson Works team 1927.
L to R. Jimmie Guthrie,
Bert Le Vack, Ted Bullus.

J. GUTHRIE.
2ND IN SENIOR T.T. 1927

Jimmie 1927. Senior T.T. second place.
(New Hudson).

Jimmie on a works New Hudson in 1927.
(Permission from Middlesbrough and District Motorcycle club to use).

1930 Junior T.T. (A.J.S.).
Signpost Corner

1930 Senior T.T.
(A.J.S.) Mountain.

1930 Lightweight T.T.
First (A.J.S.).

1930 Lightweight T.T. Jimmie Guthrie, First (A.J.S.); C.W. Johnston, Second (OK Supreme),
(Note missing exhaust pipe); C.S. Barron, Third. (OK Supreme).

Jimmie, St Andrew's Scottish Championship 1930.
(Works A.J.S.).

Jimmie, (OK Supreme), 1931 Lightweight T.T.
Braddon Bridge.

Jimmie, (Note the air deflector on the Norton.)
1931 Ulster G.P.

Jimmie, 1932 Junior Creg-ny-baa, just prior
to crashing his Norton.

Jimmie at Ballig Bridge 1932 Senior T.T. (Norton).
(Note the back tyre on landing.)

Works Norton Team 1933. L to R. Jimmy Simpson, Tim Hunt, Stanley Woods,
Jimmie Guthrie, Joe Craig.

Jimmie, (Norton), Flat out in Junior T.T. 1934.
between Quarter Bridge and Braddon.

Jimmie Guthrie Presentation by
Hawick Town Council 1934.

Jimmie, (Norton).
Junior T.T. 1935.

1935 Works Norton Team. L to R. Johnny Duncan,
Walter Rusk, Jimmie Guthrie.

Jimmie, (Norton), 1935 Swiss G.P.
Note the cobbles!

Jimmie (Norton).
Big slide at the Swiss G.P. 1935.

CHAPTER FOUR
EUROPEAN CHAMPION - AND MORE WORLD RECORDS

That year, 1935, the Ulster was also the European GP, so Guthrie was European Champion for the first time. Before winter arrived, there was still serious business to be done and Jimmie went down to Spain and a new 1½ mile GP course. Again he cleaned up in both the 350 and 500 races. The German DKW rider, Arthur Geiss, won the 150cc race and gave the Nazi salute.

And there was also the second record-breaking "jaunt" at Montlhery with Joe Craig. In fact, these sessions were far from easy. The concrete surface of the speed bowl wasn't good, and at one point it was partly iced over, the date being 22nd October. In order to do the business, the big Norton had to have its throttle held on the stop, probably at about 120 mph. The centrifugal force generated must have been formidable.

The bike's engine internals had been strengthened, it didn't have the 1934 nose cone which had probably affected the steering, but it had the huge seven-gallon tank instead of the normal 2¾ gallon one and a small megaphone exhaust to give power at the top end of the rev range.

Jimmie set off and put up a lap of 118.26 mph before being slowed by a leaking tank which splashed fuel on to his goggles. But he kept going and established a new hour record of

Jimmie passing a less-lucky competitor at Crystal Palace, May 1937.

114.09 mph. He also took the intermediate records (50km, 50mile, 100km,100mile) at over 114 mph and all five speeds beat the existing records for the 750cc and 1000cc classes.

On the Imperial Airways flight from Paris to London, Jimmie and Joe dined on roast duck, the first time a hot meal had been served on that route. The bike was rushed to the Olympia Show as the star attraction.

With Walter Rusk still sidelined through injury, the 1936 Norton works team was Jimmie, plus "Crasher" White and the gentlemanly stonemason from Grimsby, Freddie Frith. Nortons had their new rear-sprung frame and increased the 490cc engine to 499cc to extract maximum power.

A BUSY DAY

On May 3, Jimmie hanselled it with 350 and 500 class wins at the Swiss GP. The 350 race was 136 miles long, started at 8am, and Jimmie led all the way, averaging over 80 mph. Significantly, the supercharged BMW made its first appearance in the 500 event, which was run in the afternoon. Jimmie did another 30 laps to win, with a record one of 91.7 mph. That day he did 272 racing miles.

Interestingly, he had said in a rare interview granted the previous winter that supercharged bikes were a long

way off, and that the single cylinder engine would prevail. Three years later, in 1939 BMW won the Senior TT with their supercharged twin. But if it hadn't been for the brilliance of Guthrie - and later Geoff Duke - the multis might have overtaken the singles earlier.

The 1936 North West 200 in Ireland followed the Swiss GP and Jimmie won the 500. While practising for the TT, he crashed heavily at 100 mph on a bend near Cronk-y-Voddy, wrecking the bike and putting himself in hospital. He was discharged quickly but with a very stiff neck. In the race itself, he led at a cracking pace, but on the fourth lap the chain jumped the sprockets at Hillberry. He pulled in, refitted the chain and set off in pursuit of Frith.

Then they said he'd been given outside assistance by a marshall, and was black-flagged. As Motor Cycling put it "It was the most startling announcement ever made to a TT crowd. Jim Guthrie, that beloved, clever, hard-headed Scotsman had, or so they said, earned disqualification for a breach of the rules." Nortons protested. Guthrie said the marshall had pushed him down the bank but not on the road. He had finished and after an enquiry was granted fifth place but was paid for second. After a titanic struggle with Stanley Woods, who had moved to Velocettes, Guthrie also won the Senior TT by 14 seconds, at a record average of 85.80 mph.

The Grand Prix of Europe of 1936 was run in conjunction with the German GP at the Sachsenring. There was a lot of nationalistic feeling around, and Nazi salutes. Jimmie won the 500 and Norton ran a big ad afterwards "All that stood between

Great Britain and defeat in both the Senior and Junior classes of the Grand Prix of Europe was 'The Roadholder'. GP of Europe won for the fifth time in succession."

A hard one for Hitler to swallow although he was said to be a great admirer of Guthrie. After Jimmie's fatal accident, Hitler presented his mechanic with a large brass statue of Mercury. After the war it was used by the Kirkcaldy Club for the winner of the 500cc class at Beveridge Park. It is now used at Knockhill for the 600cc class. And Mrs Guthrie has a three feet long bronze trophy of three men racing on BMWs which needs two people to lift it. The inscription reads "The Grand Prix of Europe. The Leader and Chancellor of the German Reich, Adolf Hitler, 1936."

Nortons and Jimmie did it again at the Dutch TT (beating Otto Ley/BMW) and the Belgian GP, both in the 500cc class. He retired in that year's Ulster with engine trouble, and the Swedish GP didn't go well either. There, the BMWs of Ley and Gall easily beat Jimmie into third place. Top whack of the 500 Norton would be around 115mph, the blown German twins maybe 10 mph quicker - a big advantage over the better-handling Norton on a straight course. Nonetheless, in 1936, Guthrie had won five 500cc races and one 350cc and there was no question of who was still top dog.

Artist Jock Leyden went to the TT each year and sketched the interesting bikes.
Jock was a Guthrie fan. Now almost 90 he lives in South Africa.
This is his drawing of the 1934 TT Norton.

Just before the Olympia Show, Jimmie and Joe went to Montlhery for the third year running, this time taking with them a 350 as well as a 500. Jimmie broke four 350 records including the hour at 107.43 mph and was odds on to beat his own 500cc hour record of 117mph when he ran out of fuel with only a few minutes to go. Afterwards they discovered a punctured float in the carburettor. But he still took the 50km, 50mile and 100km - all at over 117 mph.

For the 1937 season, the works Nortons had more puff. Following the example of Velocettes, they now had a double overhead camshaft motor, and in the Junior TT Jimmie won at 4mph more than his old race record, and even faster than his old lap record. His speed was an average of 84.43 mph and he shared the fastest lap with Frith at 85.18 mph. It was to be his last TT victory, for although he set the pace as usual in the Senior, his engine lost compression and he stopped on the Mountain.

Nortons had called up Harold

Daniell to join Guthrie, White and Frith. Harold was so short-sighted that he failed his Army medical, despite having won the 1938 Senior TT at a record-breaking 91mph! Jimmie and Fred took on the BMWs at the Dutch TT but its long straights suited the German twins. Jimmie held them for a few laps but after lap 10 his Norton expired. Dejected, he rode straight to his hotel. The 500 Norton just didn't have enough steam.

The Swiss GP at Berne was also the venue for the 1937 Grand Prix of Europe and it was vital to get wins if at all possible. In addition to the blown BMWs, Gilera were there with their blown four-cylinder Rondine. But the 350 model of the racing Norton was still cock of the walk and Jimmie won that class at record speed. In the Senior, Gall (BMW) shot ahead, but the twisty Bremgarten circuit was in the favour of the good-handling Norton, and Jimmie won the 45-lapper at another record speed - 88.39 mph. And despite falling off on oil, he also won the 500 class of the Belgian GP.

The winner's bouquet. Jimmie, who had just won the 1937 500 Belgian GP, with second man 'Crasher" White and Joe Craig.

The smiles of the victors, (top) Team mate Tim Hunt, winner of the 1931 Junior TT, congratulates Jimmie on his fine second place. Sponsor Nigel Spring is extreme left.
(Below) Hunt then retired through injury, says "well done" to Jimmie after winning the 1936 Senior TT.

The all-conquering Norton works team of 1937 in the Island for the TT. Freddie Frith, J.H. "Crasher" White and Jimmie Guthrie.

CHAPTER FIVE
THE LAST RACE OF
A BELOVED CHAMPION

Nortons were now finding it much harder to win, faced with the challenge from the German factories, particularly BMW in the 500 class. So it was against this background that the four-man works team went to the Sachsenring for the German Grand Prix on 8 August 1937. The circuit was based on the small Saxonian town of Hohenstein-Ernstthal, away down near the border with Czechoslovakia.

The circuit was roughly a rectangle through picturesque rolling fields and woods, and the surface was close-set road-metal blocks. Guthrie knew it well for he had been several times, and had won the previous year. He was hugely popular with the Germans, 250,000 of whom had turned up. There was a soldier every five yards round the circuit and 50 doctors and seven dentists. Jimmie (40) was the oldest rider in the race.

The 500 was the last event of the day. On the front row of the grid were Jimmie Guthrie (Norton), who was the reigning Champion of Europe, Ley (BMW), Mansfeld (DKW), and Gall (BMW). In the second row were Frith (Norton), Tenni (Guzzi), Bodmer (DKW) and Stanley Woods (Guzzi). On lap 4, Jimmie took the lead from Ley and established a healthy gap of 1½ minutes. Craig signalled him to ease. He had no trouble in

maintaining his lead and went into the last lap with two minutes to spare.

The Union Jack was readied and it was going to be a popular victory. But the minutes passed and there was no sign of Guthrie. Then second man Gall, the German, appeared and took the winner's flag. There was virtual silence. When the news came, it was bad. Guthrie had crashed while overtaking another competitor and was very seriously injured.

This is where it all passes into conjecture. Until 1992, several versions were put forward. One was that the rear spindle, drilled for lightness, had broken or had come out, and that Guthrie had fought the machine, minus its back wheel, which had been found up a tree. A picture exists which shows the Norton in the ditch, battered and without its rear wheel. Anyone who has seen a motor cycle crash at speed will know that the wheel could easily come out as a result of the impact. But the theory is credible.

So is the one that the engine ran out of oil, seized, and locked the back wheel. These Norton engines did use a lot of oil, but an engine seizure on a four-stroke can be remedied by whipping in the clutch. In fact, the big-end was seized, as it would be if a bike is lying in a ditch and revving its guts out. There is no record of the gearbox being locked up, which would've been a different matter.

The only eye-witness was Stanley

The immaculate style of Jimmie Guthrie at Sachsenring, 8 August 1937.

Woods. At the end of a long life when he was still totally sharp he gave an interview to Mick Woollett for his book "Norton". This was in 1992. Why he didn't come out with his revelation before, nobody will know. Maybe it was in deference to Mrs Guthrie's feelings, or maybe nobody ever asked him. Gordon Small knew Stanley well and questioned him closely, but Stanley was adamant.

"I am prepared to go on oath that Guthrie was fouled. I saw the accident because I was coasting to halt with a broken petrol pipe. Two riders passed me, a German and Guthrie. It was just before a downhill right-hander which Jimmie took flat out. The German knew Guthrie was right behind him, for he'd been there for some time. But the German couldn't take it flat out, slackened, and pulled into Jimmie's path, forcing him off the road into a line of saplings. He ended up in the foot of a ditch.

"I was the first to reach him and could see that he was in a desperately bad way. Both legs and an arm were broken. But he had no head injuries. I don't think he knew he was dying. I went in the ambulance with him to hospital, but the roads were choked and it took two hours.

"After 20 minutes or so, the surgeon came out and said that they'd revived him momentarily, but that he had died. You can imagine how I felt. We'd been friends, team-mates and rivals for ten years. I was shattered."

The German rider was Kurt Mansfeld, who had been a lap behind Guthrie, but he was known as a headstrong and emotional man, not popular even with the Germans. It's not suggested that there was any nationalistic feeling about it, or even that it was done intentionally. The best that can be said is that he thought he could show Guthrie how to do it, couldn't get round the bend, panicked, and shut off.

He has his defenders. Former World Champion Bill Lomas told Gordon Small that he knew Mansfeld in the '50s and he always denied everything. Said he was nowhere near. Lomas accepted this. Austrian historian, Prof. Helmut Krackowizer says an old rider, Faistenhammer, told him he wasn't far behind and although he saw nothing, he smelled burning rubber which he took to be from Guthrie's locked wheel.

Mrs Guthrie is reserved about it, but one gets the impression that she believes a third party was involved. It is all a long time ago. It is said that the Saxons are without sentiment except for horses, dogs and war comrades lost. They were desolate about Jimmie Guthrie, for they loved him dearly. He lay in state, a soldier at each corner of his bier, until arrangements could be made to take him back to Scotland. The train was given a military escort to the German frontier.

But what about poor Mrs Guthrie? " The first I knew that Jimmie had been killed was when a reporter came to the door. Later, I heard it on the radio. Margaret was two at the time and I was carrying Jimmie. He was born in the October." With the acceptance which comes with time, she says:

"It isn't worth it, you know. The risk isn't worth it. When young Jimmie grew up it was in his blood too, but I never stood in his way. I was in the Isle of Man when he won the Senior Manx Grand Prix on a Francis Beart Norton. After that win, he stopped

SCENES FROM HIS LAST RACE. . . . .

◀ Joe Craig tests a plug. Note the cobble-stones.

The start — ▶
Guthrie, Ley
Mansfeld, Gall.

◀ Part of the circuit and the huge crowd.

The last picture ▶
taken of Guthrie,
a lap ahead, as
he leads
Mansfeld.

racing and went out to work in South Africa.

"I have been out there many times to visit him and I often go down to see Margaret and her family in Devon. We are all close and get on well together. Jimmie - and Margaret - take a great interest in their father's achievements."

Jimmie's funeral in Hawick was attended by thousands, many of whom lined the streets, bareheaded men weeping unashamedly. It was like a Welsh mining disaster epitomised in one man. The cortege was three miles long and the Guthrie's large garden was quite literally covered in wreaths, which had spilled out from the house. The coffin was wrapped in the Union Jack which waited for him in vain at the German finishing line. Among the pallbearers were his team mates from Nortons - Craig, Frith, Simpson and Woods.

Within days, The Motor Cycle had opened their Shilling Fund, whereby the public could contribute what they could afford to the memorial to be erected at The Cutting, the spot where he had stopped in his last Isle of Man TT, the Senior of 1937. From there, one can see Scotland on a clear day. The concluding sentence on the plaque reads: "He died while upholding the honour of his country in the German Grand Prix, August, 1937."

Another public subscription resulted in the erection in 1939 of the magnificent Thomas Clapperton statue in Wilton Park, Hawick, only a few yards from the museum.

But perhaps most touching of all is the memorial erected by the Saxons in 1949. They invited Mrs Guthrie and Jimmie out to see it in 1967 and she was given the warmest of welcomes by the huge crowd. She found it an almost overwhelmingly emotional occasion and she is in touch with them still. Despite the ongoing generations,

there is still a kind of Guthrie appreciation society, which was brought home to Gordon Small when he went there on his own motor cycle in 1993. He says:

"The memorial is a large and rough stone set down in the ditch where he finished up. It has a plaque about 'our friend Jimmie Guthrie.' The saplings he hit are big now, and the cobbled surface of the road is tarred and smooth.

"Quite a lot of traffic goes by, but there are quiet periods too, and during one of these I stood and reflected on Jimmie and what he had achieved. I thought of Scotland and how far away it was for me, but how much further it would've been for him. The visit was a kind of homage which I'd promised myself to do for a long time. I was quite overcome.

"The Guthrie Stone, as it is known, is surrounded by a little fence, inside which is a garden, the size of a living room, and beautifully kept on a regular basis. There were planted flowers, posies and formal wreaths with coloured ribbons. In my schoolboy German I left a note 'Thank you for remembering Jimmie Guthrie - a Scottish motorcyclist' and my address.

"A few weeks later I got a letter from a lady, Frau Karin Schettler, and in 1996 I visited her in the family home which looks over the old Sachsenring and up to the woods to where it all happened. Frau Schettler told me that her father had taken it upon himself to look after The Guthrie Stone and now she - in middle age - has taken on the mantle. She says that in summer, flowers with messages of goodwill, appear from all over the world. It is a recognised meeting place not only for local riders but motorcyclists from all over Europe."

Jimmie Guthrie would be pleased about that.

The Guthrie Stone in Germany.

JIMMIE GUTHRIE
An Appreciation from 1937

*A*nd so Jimmie Guthrie is dead. He has run his last race and won his last victory. Within a short mile from the winning post, and the prize within his grasp, the flag has fallen. The applause of the multitude is hushed, but for him surely the greater reward. The race of Life well run, his is the "Well done, good and faithful servant".

We knew him affectionately as "Jimmie," a testimonial to his simplicity of character, and the esteem in which we held him. The great modesty with which he bore his laurels — a world wide fame which might have turned anyone's head — left him unspoiled. His was the true greatness... to do great deeds and win great successes and still remain the same simple and unassuming man he was. It was this which endeared him so much to all who knew him — it is for this we honour him today.

Some years ago when Jimmie lay so long in the Cottage Hospital, we thought his racing days were over — but they were only beginning. His great heart carried him through despite everything — and only death itself could end his career.

The world admires a brave man, and so upon his grave will be laid greater laurels than even he has won... the tribute of his fellow men to the loving memory of one whom they admired for his character and worth.

CHAPTER SIX

HIS MAJOR ROAD RACING ACHIEVEMENTS

1927 — 2nd Senior TT. (works New Hudson)

1928 — 2nd 350 German Grand Prix, 2nd 350 Swiss Grand Prix. (both works Norton)

1930 — 1st Lightweight TT, 1st 350 German Grand Prix. (both A.J.S.)

1931 — The following were all on works Nortons. 2nd Junior TT, 2nd Senior TT, 3rd 500 French Grand Prix, 1st 500 at Solitude (Germany), 1st 350 Belgian Grand Prix, 2nd 350 Ulster Grand Prix.

1932 — 1st 350 Leinster "200", 2nd Senior TT, 2nd 350 Belgian Grand Prix.

1933 — 3rd Junior TT, 4th Senior TT, 2nd 350 French Grand Prix, 1st 350 Belgian Grand Prix, 2nd 350 Ulster Grand Prix, 1st 350 Spanish Grand Prix, 1st 500 Spanish Grand Prix, 2nd 350 Grand Prix of Europe (Sweden).

1934 — 1st Junior TT, 1st Senior TT.

1935 — 1st 500 North West "200", 1st Junior TT, 2nd Senior TT, 1st 500 Swiss Grand Prix, 2nd 350 Swiss Grand Prix, 1st 500 Dutch TT, 1st 500 German Grand Prix, 1st 500 Belgian Grand Prix, 1st 500 Grand Prix of Europe (Ulster), 1st 350 Spanish Grand Prix, 1st 500 Spanish Grand Prix.

1936 — 1st 350 Swiss Grand Prix, 1st 500 Swiss Grand Prix, 1st 500 North West "200", 1st Senior TT, 1st 500 Belgian Grand Prix, 1st 500 Grand Prix of Europe (Germany), 1st 500 Dutch TT, 3rd 500 Swedish Grand Prix.

1937 — 1st 350 Leinster "200",1st 500 North West "200", 1st Junior TT, 1st 350 Grand Prix of Europe, 1st 500 Grand Prix of Europe (both Switzerland), 1st 500 Belgian Grand Prix.

WORLD SPEED RECORDS AT MONTLHERY, FRANCE.

1934 — 50km record at 113.23mph, 50 miles record at 113.39 mph, both records using a 490 Norton.

1935 — One hour record at 114.09 mph. The world 50 km, 50 miles, 100km and 100 miles were all beaten at over 114 mph. All five figures also beat the existing records for the 750 and 1000cc classes. All riding a 490 Norton.

1936 — One hour 350cc record at 107.43 mph (348 Norton). World 50km, 50 miles, 100km records broken at over 117 mph (490 Norton).

● *Hawick Archaeological Society would like to thank D.C. Thomson and Co. Ltd, Prof. Helmut Krackowizer, The Goddard Collection, and Messrs Alec Waldie, Jack Fraser, Jim Millar and Carlisle Reid.*
Jimmie Guthrie — Hawick's Racing Legend ©. Gordon Small 1997.

"Deep respect and grief at the loss of one so great and noble prompts the NORTON Company to publish this for you to retain — in memory."

This picture was given in 1937 to anyone who had any connection with Nortons.

Produced by Core 3 Partners Ltd. Carnarvon Street, Hawick, Scotland